Dale Earnhardt Jr.

Revised Edition

By Jeff Savage

AMAZING ATHLETES

Lerner Publications • Minneapolis

Lerner Publications Company
A division of Lerner Publishing Group, Inc.
241 First Avenue North
Minneapolis, MN 55401 USA

For reading levels and more information, look up this title at www.lernerbooks.com.

Library of Congress Cataloging-in-Publication Data

Savage, Jeff, 1961–
  Dale Earnhardt Jr. / by Jeff Savage. — 2nd Revised Edition.
    pages   cm. — (Amazing Athletes)
  Includes index.
  Audience: Age: 7–11.
  ISBN 978-1-4677-7583-0 (pbk : alk. paper) — ISBN 978-1-4677-7585-4 (EB pdf)
  1. Earnhardt, Dale, Jr.—Juvenile literature. 2. Automobile racing drivers—United States—Biography—Juvenile literature. 3. Automobile racing drivers—Biography. I. Title. II. Title: Dale Earnhardt Junior.
  GV1032.E19S28 2015
  796.72092—dc23 [B]   2014032125

Manufactured in the United States of America
1 – BP – 12/31/14

TABLE OF CONTENTS

Fans watch the cars round a bend during the 2014 Daytona 500.

DAYTONA DOUBLE

The green flag snapped in the wind. Dale Earnhardt Jr. roared down the track in his race car. He was surrounded on all sides by other cars. Cameras flashed and rain clouds rolled overhead. The 2014 Daytona 500 was under way!

The Daytona 500 is the most important race of the NASCAR season. Fans call it the Great American Race. It is held each year at Daytona International Speedway in Daytona Beach, Florida. The Daytona 500 is one of the most watched car races of the year. It also has the largest purse of the NASCAR season. In 2014, the purse was more than $19 million!

Dale's car *(bottom)* races down the track.

Dale's car *(bottom center)* is caught in a pack.

Dale was stuck in the middle of a pack of cars early in the race. But he didn't panic. Dale had won the Daytona 500 in 2004. He knew that a lot could change during the 200-**lap** race. There was plenty of time to break free. He kept steady hands on the steering wheel and looked for open space.

As the racers sped through their 38th lap, rain poured from the sky. Fans in the **grandstand** ran for shelter. Out came the **red flag**. The race was stopped until the rain passed.

The first Daytona 500 took place in 1959. Lee Petty won the race by two feet.

Workers pump water off the track during the rain delay.

The delay lasted more than six hours. Finally, a race official waved the green flag again. The Daytona 500 was back on! Dale cruised to the front of the pack. He took the lead for the first time on lap 131. But he couldn't stay in front. The lead changed dozens of times as the cars sped toward the 200th lap.

Drivers began to take more risks as they neared the finish line. They couldn't wait any longer to try to take the lead. The risky driving led to a crash with multiple cars. Dale escaped the pileup. He was in first place after the crashed cars were cleared from the track. He held the lead for two more laps, avoided another crash, and crossed the finish line. A race official waved the **checkered flag**. Dale had his second Daytona 500 victory. It was time to celebrate!

Dale *(left)* crosses the finish line to win the 2014 Daytona 500.

Dale drove around the track with the checkered flag streaming from his race car window. Fans clapped and cheered and snapped photos. After his lap, Dale headed to **Victory Lane**. He hugged one of his **crew members**. Then Dale and his entire crew came together for a group hug. **Confetti** rained down as Dale raised both his arms in the air.

Dale took home more than $1.5 million in **prize money**. But the victory was about more than money for the racer. He hadn't reached Victory Lane in any race since 2012. His recent struggles made this win all the sweeter. "This is better than the first one!" Dale said.

Dale celebrates his victory with members of his crew.

Dale *(left)* with his father, Dale Earnhardt Sr. Dale Sr. was one of NASCAR's greatest drivers.

LEARNING TO RACE

Dale Earnhardt Jr. was born October 10, 1974, in Concord, North Carolina. His mother's name is Brenda Earnhardt. Dale Jr.'s parents divorced when he was three years old. So Dale and his older sister Kelley lived with their mother.

When Dale was six, a fire destroyed his mother's home. Dale and Kelley went to live with their father in Kannapolis, North Carolina. Dale also lived with his stepmother Teresa. Later, his half brother Kerry and stepsister Taylor Nicole joined the family.

Dale grew up around race cars and racetracks. His father was NASCAR's most popular driver. Dale Earnhardt Sr.'s tough, hard-charging style earned him the nickname the Intimidator. Dale's grandfather Ralph Earnhardt was also a top race car driver who won many races.

Dale's nickname was Junior. He loved watching races on TV.

Dale Earnhardt Sr. won the **points title** seven times. He is tied with Richard Petty for having the most points titles.

Dale's father let his son make his own decisions. "But he always had one eye on me," Dale said. After Dale got his driver's license, he and his half brother bought a 1978 Chevrolet Monte Carlo for $200. They fixed the car up to race. Dale wanted to be a race car driver for one reason. "I wanted to impress my dad," he admitted.

Dale's half brother, Kerry, was also a successful NASCAR driver.

Dale Sr. did not want to help his sons too much. He wanted his boys to learn about cars and racing on their own. "He's got to learn it from the bottom up," Dale Earnhardt Sr. said. "How far up he goes is based on how much he learns." Dale Jr. was not allowed to race the car until he drove it for 150 laps without stopping. One day, Dale did so. "Well," his father said, "you didn't hit anything. Let's see how you do in traffic."

It didn't take long for Dale to show he was ready to be a NASCAR driver.

A ROARING START

Dale's racing career soared from the start. He started racing when he was 17 years old. Soon he was competing at tracks in North and South Carolina.

When Dale wasn't racing, he worked at his father's car dealership. But his favorite place was the racetrack. Meanwhile, Dale's dad kept an eye on him. Dale Sr. saw that his son was an excellent driver. He thought that Dale Jr. had a chance to be a success in NASCAR.

In 1998, Dale Sr. invited his son to join his team. Dale Jr. was about to get his chance to be a NASCAR driver! He started at the middle level of the racing **circuit**. The **Busch Series** was one step below NASCAR's top circuit.

Dale was nervous during his first race. He didn't do well. In fact, he got into a terrible crash. His car did a flip and landed on its wheels. Luckily, Dale was not hurt.

But Dale learned from his mistakes. Just two months later, he won his first Busch race.

Dale Sr. *(right)* congratulates his son for winning his second mid-level points title.

He earned that first victory at the Coca-Cola 300 at Texas Motor Speedway.

Dale soon won again. And again. In fact, Dale won seven races. His great season earned him the 1998 points title. He was the champion of the mid-level circuit! It was the first time in NASCAR history that a grandfather, a father, and a son had all won points titles.

In 1999, Dale won six races and the Busch Series title again. Dad was proud. "He had a lot of pressure on him," said Dale Sr. "He kept his head about him. He did a good job."

Racing fans expected big things from Dale when he joined NASCAR's top circuit.

Dale joined the top level of NASCAR in 2000. He was thrilled to race against his father and the best stock car drivers in the world. He drove with a yellow stripe on the back of his number 8 car. The stripe was a sign that he was a **rookie**.

Dale soon showed that he was ready for the top NASCAR circuit. He earned his first victory in his 12th race of the season. After Dale won the DirecTV 500 at Texas Motor Speedway, his father greeted him in Victory Lane. It was an exciting moment for both father and son.

Dale won twice more in his rookie season. He had proved his skill behind the wheel. But some people said Dale did not work hard enough at his sport. He liked to go boating and hang out with friends. "I never told anybody that I was going to be as good as my dad," said Junior. "I just want to drive race cars and make a living doing it." But then something happened that changed Dale's life forever.

Dale and his dad pose for a picture before the start of a special race at Daytona International Speedway in 2001. Dale Sr. died in a crash at Daytona just a few weeks later.

MOVING ON

Dale's life-changing moment came during the first race of the 2001 season. The 2001 Daytona 500 was a fight to the finish. On the final lap, Dale Jr. was battling Michael Waltrip for the victory. Waltrip was in first place, with Dale right behind him. Dale's father was third.

Waltrip beat out Dale Jr. for the win. But a horrible crash took place behind them. Dale Sr.'s black number 3 car had smashed into the concrete wall. Dale Sr. was killed instantly.

The racing world was shocked. NASCAR had lost its greatest driver. Dale Jr. was in shock too. In a second, he had lost his dad forever.

Dale and his stepmom Teresa get ready to speak to news reporters after Dale Sr.'s death.

Dale tried to appear strong. "We will get through this," he told reporters. "I'm sure he would want us to keep going, and that is what we are going to do."

Dale was hurting inside. But he continued to race. It was hard. Every week, fans asked him to sign pictures of his father. Before each race, NASCAR held ceremonies for Dale Sr. At the same time, TV cameras zoomed in on Dale Jr. The attention made it hard for Dale to sort out his feelings.

Fans place flowers and gifts on one of Dale Earnhardt Sr.'s cars. Racing fans around the country were shocked and saddened by Dale Sr.'s death.

Dale celebrates a victory at the Pepsi 400 at Daytona International Speedway. It was Dale's first race at Daytona since his father's death.

"The attention, the pressure, the questions . . . it had to be unbearable," said superstar racer Jeff Gordon. Gordon won the points title that year. Dale finished in eighth place. He earned $5.8 million in prize money.

Through it all, Dale became one of NASCAR's most popular drivers. He was on talk shows. He made ads for car parts, razors, and rental cars. He even acted in TV shows and took batting practice at Major League Baseball's All-Star Game.

But Dale's performance did not match his popularity. In 2002, he finished in 11th place. Early in the season, he injured his head in a crash. He drove poorly in the next several races. But Dale did not make excuses. It was time for him to do better.

Dale *(center)* celebrates after winning the 2004 Daytona 500.

RACING STAR

Dale worked hard. In 2003 and 2004, he finished in the top five in the points standings. He won six races and $8.9 million in prize money in 2004. But the biggest win of the year came at the Daytona 500. Dale took the top spot at the race where his dad had lost his life three years earlier. "He was over in the passenger side riding with me," Dale said of his father. "I'm sure he was having a blast."

Dale celebrates a victory in his number 8 car.

Ever since Dale Jr. started racing stock cars, he'd been part of the Dale Earnhardt, Inc. (DEI) racing company. Dale Sr. and his wife Teresa had started DEI when Dale Jr. was just five years old. Driving for the company had been a way for Dale Jr. to be close to his dad. But the team didn't feel the same without Dale Sr.

In 2007, Dale announced that he was leaving DEI. It was time to move on. He joined Hendrick Motorsports as the driver of their number 88 car.

The move didn't slow him down. Dale won the first two races of the 2008 season.

Dale won many races and competed for points titles over the following years. In 2010, he finished second at the Daytona 500. He finished second again in 2012 and 2013. But Dale had a higher goal in mind. He'd already won the 500 once. He knew he could do it again.

Dale leads the pack during a race in 2012.

Dale's luck changed at the 2014 Daytona 500. He took the top spot at the Great American Race for the second time. Dale remembered feeling proud after winning the Daytona 500 in 2004. He felt the same in 2014. "That [feeling] will last forever," Dale said. "You never forget about it." Dale is young enough to keep racing for many years. Maybe he'll win the Daytona 500 again. But even if he doesn't, Dale has become a racing star that NASCAR fans will never forget.

Dale greets fans before a 2014 race.

Selected Career Highlights

2014 Won the Daytona 500 for the second time

2013 Finished fifth in the Sprint Cup points standings
Won NASCAR's Most Popular Driver Award for the 11th time

2012 Finished 12th in the Sprint Cup points standings
Won NASCAR's Most Popular Driver Award for the 10th time

2011 Finished seventh in the Sprint Cup points standings
Won NASCAR's Most Popular Driver Award for the ninth time

2010 Finished 21st in the Sprint Cup points standings
Won NASCAR's Most Popular Driver Award for the eighth time

2009 Finished 25th in the Sprint Cup points standings
Won NASCAR's Most Popular Driver Award for the seventh time

2008 Finished 12th in the Sprint Cup points standings
Won NASCAR's Most Popular Driver Award for the sixth time

2007 Finished 16th in the Sprint Cup points standings
Won NASCAR's Most Popular Driver Award for the fifth time

2006 Finished fifth in the Sprint Cup points standings
Won NASCAR's Most Popular Driver Award for the fourth time

2005 Finished 19th in the Sprint Cup points standings
Won NASCAR's Most Popular Driver Award for the third time

2004 Finished fifth in the Sprint Cup points standings
Won the Daytona 500
Won NASCAR's Most Popular Driver Award for the second time

2003 Finished third in the Sprint Cup points standings
Won NASCAR's Most Popular Driver Award

2002 Finished 11th in the Sprint Cup points standings

2001 Finished eighth in the Sprint Cup Cup points standings

2000 Won the DirecTV 500 at Texas Motor Speedway for
his first Sprint Cup victory

1999 Won the Busch Series title for the
second time

1998 Won the Busch Series title
Won seven Busch Series races

Glossary

Busch Series: NASCAR's second circuit. Busch Series drivers hope to earn a spot in NASCAR's top circuit, the Sprint Cup. Since 2008, the Busch Series has been called the Nationwide Series.

checkered flag: the black-and-white flag that is waved at the end of a race

circuit: a racing league

confetti: small, colored pieces of paper that are thrown or dropped during a celebration

crew members: people who build and repair NASCAR cars and trucks

grandstand: the area at a racetrack where fans watch a NASCAR race

green flag: a flag waved by a NASCAR official at the beginning of a race or after a delay

lap: a complete trip around a racetrack

NASCAR: the National Association for Stock Car Auto Racing. Founded in 1947, NASCAR is the governing group of stock car racing. It says which changes to a car's engine and body are allowed to make it a stock car.

points standings: a list that shows how many points each NASCAR driver has earned. The driver with the most points is at the top of the standings. The driver with the second-most points is second in the standings and so on.

points title: an award given each year to the NASCAR driver who has earned the most points throughout the racing season. In NASCAR, drivers earn points for winning races, finishing well in races, and for other reasons.

prize money: the money awarded to each driver based on the driver's finish in a race

purse: the total amount of money offered as a prize for a race. Drivers split up the purse depending on what place they are in when they finish the race.

red flag: a flag waved by an official at a NASCAR race that signals the race must be stopped

rookie: a first-year player or driver in a sport or league

Victory Lane: a road extending from the racetrack that the winning car drives along when celebrating a win

Further Reading & Websites

Howell, Brian. *Rally Car Racing: Tearing It Up*. Minneapolis: Lerner Publications, 2014.

Roe Pimm, Nancy. *The Daytona 500: The Thrill and Thunder of the Great American Race*. Minneapolis: Millbrook Press, 2011.

Savage, Jeff. *Jeff Gordon*. Minneapolis: Lerner Publications, 2007.

NASCAR.com
http://www.nascar.com/en_us/sprint-cup-series.html
NASCAR's official site has recent news stories, driver biographies, and information about racing teams and stock cars.

The Official Website of Dale Earnhardt Jr.
http://www.dalejr.com/default.aspx
Dale's official website features trivia, photos, information, and occasional letters from Dale.

Sports Illustrated Kids
http://www.sikids.com
The *Sports Illustrated Kids* website covers all sports, including NASCAR.

LERNER

Expand learning beyond the printed book. Download free, complementary educational resources for this book from our website, www.lerneresource.com.

SOURCE

Index

Photo Acknowledgments

The images in this book are used with the permission of: © Jonathan Ferrey/NASCAR via Getty Images, p. 4; © Robert Laberge/Getty Images, pp. 5, 6; AP Photo/NKP, Russell LaBounty, p. 7; © Chris Trotman/NASCAR via Getty Images, p. 9; © Tom Pennington/Getty Images, p. 10; REUTERS/Joe Skipper, p. 11; © Harold Hinson/The Sporting News/ZUMA Press, p. 13; © Brian Cleary/Getty Images, p. 15; © Brian Cleary/Icon SMI, p. 17; © Duomo/CORBIS, p. 18; REUTERS/Mark Wallheiser, p. 20; REUTERS/Steve Marcus, p. 21; REUTERS/Tami Chappell, p. 22; REUTERS/Charles W Luzier, p. 23; © ISC Archives/Getty Images, p. 25; © George Tiedemann/GT Images/CORBIS, p. 26; AP Photo/Autostock, Russell LaBounty, p. 27; © Chris Grathen/NASCAR via Getty Images, pp. 28, 29.

Front cover: © Jamie Squire/NASCAR viaGetty Images.

Main body text set in Caecilia LT Std 55 Roman 16/28.
Typeface provided by Adobe Systems.